MW01629239
W
E
S
MAUI
LĀNA'I
HAWAI'I
KAHO'OLAWE

Dedications

To Paul, Jack, and Liam -
The inspiration for this book and my travel buddies forever.

- E.J.

To the islands that inspire art, an appreciation of its culture, and admiration of its beauty every day.

- K.P.S.

175 Kahelu Avenue, Unit #4
Mililani, Hawai'i 96789
Orders: (800) 468-2800
Information: (808) 564-8800
Fax: (808) 564-8877
welcometotheislands.com

ISBN: 1-61710-479-5
First Edition, First Printing — 2020
COP 200701

OUR HAWAI'I VACATION

Written by Elizabeth Janczyk
Illustrated by Kristi Petosa-Sigel

ISLAND HERITAGE®

The busy year now has passed,
our **HAWAI'I** vacation is here at last!

April
May
June
Hawaii!

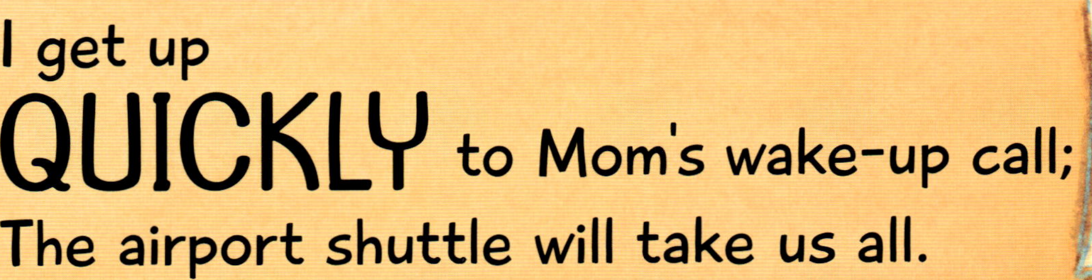

I get up **QUICKLY** to Mom's wake-up call;
The airport shuttle will take us all.

My Family

The travel day has FINALLY arrived;
My swimsuit is packed.

It's time to FLY!

It's Mommy, Daddy, Brother, and me,
Plus Grandma and Grandpa, my whole FAMILY.

We check our BAGS and wait in line,
Through the scanner, we all are fine!

We meet our pilot (that is neat),
then board the PLANE and take our seats.

Taking off and climbing the SKY,

Like a giant **BIRD,** we fly.

The plane lands on the RUNWAY
and drives to the gate;
We are right on time, not a minute late.

Now that we're here,
there's so much fun to be had,
I especially love building
SANDCASTLES
with Dad!

We ride a TRAIN and tour a plantation,
then eat shave ice —
what a delicious vacation!

SHAVE ICE

Beach time is fun,
with lots of sand between our toes;
Maybe we'll take a boat ride or go to
a LUAU — who knows!?

Island life is so FUN and free,
playing in waves and under palm trees.

Surf, sand, wind and sea,
I love spending TIME with my family!

Every year
I look forward to this family vacation;
the HAWAIIAN ISLANDS
are my favorite location!

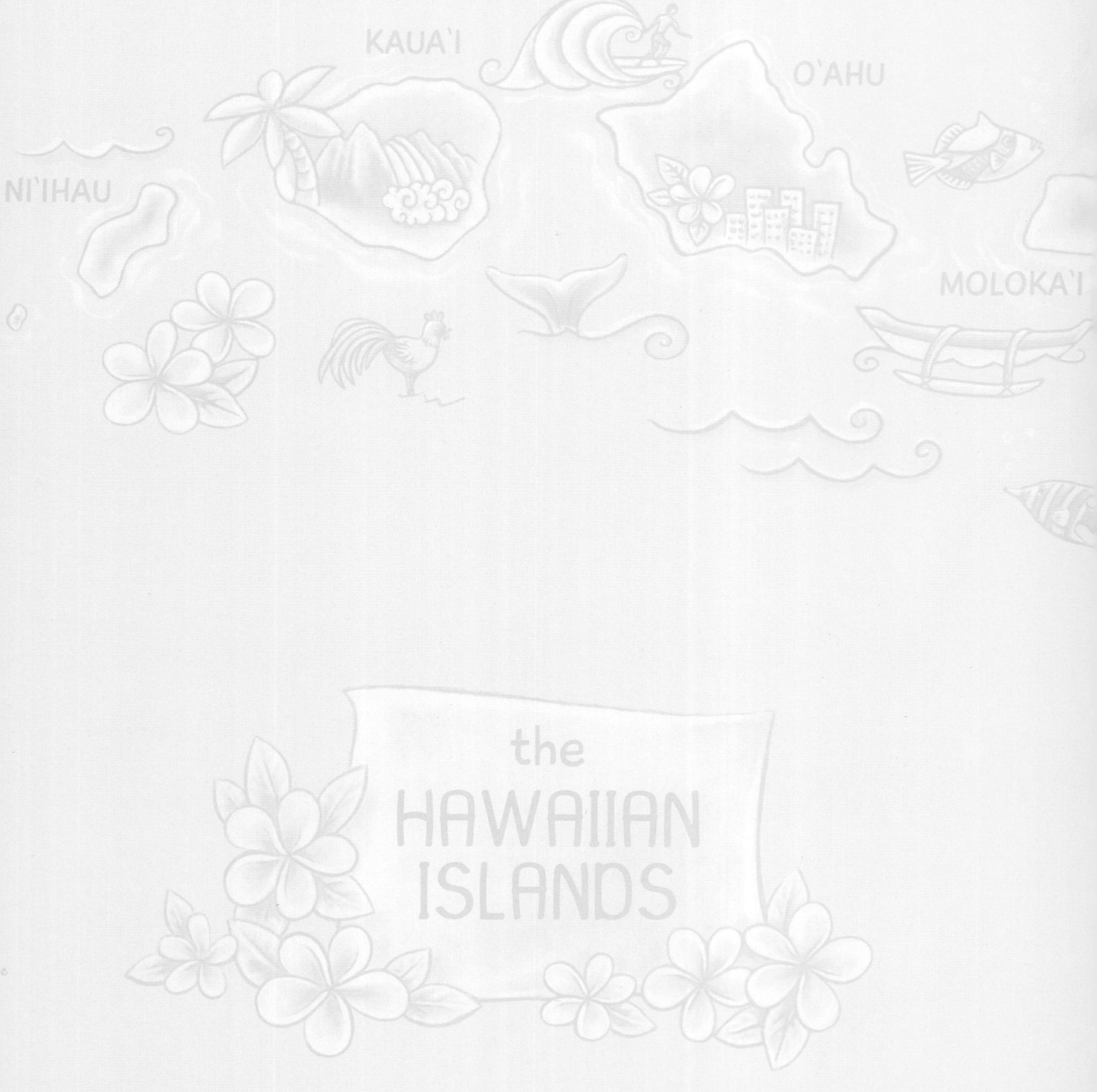

KAUA'I

O'AHU

NI'IHAU

MOLOKA'I